IMAGES
of America

GAY AND LESBIAN
WASHINGTON, D.C.

Two couples walk together in 19th-century homoaffection near the intersection of 10th and Pennsylvania in Washington, D.C.

IMAGES
of America

GAY AND LESBIAN
WASHINGTON, D.C.

Frank Muzzy

ARCADIA

Published by Arcadia Publishing
Charleston SC, Chicago IL, Portsmouth NH, San Francisco CA

Printed in Great Britain

Library of Congress Catalog Card Number: 2004112836

For all general information contact Arcadia Publishing at:
Telephone 843-853-2070
Fax 843-853-0044
E-mail sales@arcadiapublishing.com
For customer service and orders:
Toll-Free 1-888-313-2665

Visit us on the internet at http://www.arcadiapublishing.com

Dr. Mary Walker greets a fellow Washingtonian on a D.C. street. Walker was quite comfortable wearing men's attire and always proudly wore her Medal of Honor until her death.

CONTENTS

Acknowledgments   6

Introduction   7

1.   The Political Side of D.C.: "Abstracted Manor"   9

2.   Community Voices   31

3.   "Silence=Death"   63

4.   Gay Migration   79

5.   Gathering Places: "The Gays of Our Lives"   97

ACKNOWLEDGMENTS

The Rainbow History Project is an important recorder of the GLBT (Gay, Lesbian, Bisexual, and Transgender) family stories and has been an enormous service to this project, with the added blessings of Rainbow History Project director Mark Meinke, as well as the photographers of the community. Foremost on this list is Patsy Lynch, who not only opened up her photo archives, but her personal recollections as well, and has therefore helped save gay history. Other photographers who were also there for the task include Ward Morrison, Kay Tobin Lahusen, David Kosoko, and Luis Gomez. Todd Franson and Randy Shulman of *Metro Weekly* contributed photos and information. Brian Moylan of the *Washington Blade* harvested material, and several of the *Blade*'s former staff members also contributed: thank you Don Hinckle, Leigh H. Mosley, Jim Marks, David Williams, and most especially, John Yanson. There are the private collections, family albums opened and gladly shared, by Ted Goldsborough and his family, Earl Parker, Charlie Hopwood, John Copes, Barrett Brick, Frank Nowicki, Frank Asher, David Burgdorf, Buddy Sutson, Hank Becker, and Clarence J. Fluker. I would also like to thank Doug Jefferies and Sarah Lengyel French of Results, the Gym (the workouts help clear my brain); Deacon Maccubbin of Lambda Rising; Schelli Dittmann with the DC Eagle archives; Danny Linden and his Centaur MC Yearbook; Jason Hendrix, International Mr. Leather; Cornelius Baker, Andy Litsky, Chris Davies, and Robyn Robbins of Whitman-Walker Clinic and LSP; Ryan Shepard of the City Museum of Washington, D.C.; The Anthropologic Society of the Smithsonian; The National Archives; and the "granddaddy of all archival photo research" (who's your daddy?), The Library of Congress, whose accommodating staff includes Jennifer Brathovde, Maja Keech, Jeff Bridgers, Lewis Wyman, and photographers Bob Dardano and Rick Keagan.

Many writers have also saved history and authored must-reads for Gay Washington history. Ina Russell preserved her uncle's diary in *Jeb and Dash*; a special thanks goes to playwright Mark Conley for putting me in touch with her. Other important works include Mark Herlong's essays on Dr. John McCalla Jr. and Mariette Pathy Allen's book *The Gender Frontier*. Equally important are Jack Nichols's many books on the Mattachine Society, as well as *I Have More Fun with You than Anyone*, about his relationship with Lige Clarke. Interestingly, his recollections about his high school companion, Janet Welch, turned out to be a dear friend of mine, Jan Welch.

This corralling of gay history could not have happened without numerous supporters and those who simply encouraged me. Bob Marquart at Arcadia Publishing suggested me for this project, while editors extraordinaire Susan Beck and Kathryn Korfonta were kind listeners who laughed at all the right places. Of course, I thank everyone at Pulp on 14th and Pulp on the Hill. Without a doubt, however, this could not have materialized without the 24/7 in my life, who is more than a computer expert, more than a photographer, more than an editor/translator of thoughts, more than a colleague, more than a special friend, and with whom, along the way, "I have more fun with than anyone," Michael P. Elder.

There are numerous details within the broad stroke of the Washington, D.C. GLBT community. This work has brought me many new friends in the community and reminded me how diverse it is. And I promise those friends, I will never again end my sentences with, "Do you have any photos?"

I dedicate this work to Ameda Lambert Muzzy, an extraordinary woman, actress, writer, businesswoman, confidant, supporter in all things, and mother. Je t'aime.

INTRODUCTION

The story of Gay D.C. is rich with characters and historical anecdotes. They are brought to life over a 200-year span that may shake some of historians' homogenized views.

As the foundations of the new city were to be laid, the designs were spread out by Pierre L'Enfant, by all accounts an "affected" man, an 18th-century term that implies a late 19th-century word, homosexual.

The level of intimacy between same-sex individuals of the day involves a bit of speculation, especially in discussing the sexuality of historical figures in contemporary terms. In the 19th century Pre-Freudian vernacular, love between people of the same sex did not necessarily imply eros. Of course, often it did, but in only the politest manner. Homoaffection, a male-to-male bonding as in military or sports, and its counterpart in the women's community, women-identified woman, is not necessarily sexual but rather preferring to live or be in the company of others of the same sex.

Not until 1869, while arguing for the repeal of sodomy laws in Prussia, did Karl Maria Benkert introduce the term "homosexuality" in discussing "inverts." Theories about the origins of the word "gay" in connection with same-sex attraction vary. In Victorian times, female and male prostitutes were called gay, for they were to dress gaily for business. Eventually, a boy for the night became a "gay" boy, meaning homosexual. Another theory about the term is that it evolved from the hobo community where an older, more experienced hobo provided guidance and protection for a young hobo, known as a "geycat" or "gay cat." The relationship was implicitly sexual. Prior to this terminology, we can only interpret homosexuality through familiar and descriptive words or decipher letters filled with tender references.

The city grew with many gay and lesbian influences, and its history contains both told and untold tales. These are just some of those tales depicted in photo and word. Washington's early political theater was a bit on the intriguing side, revealing that having that special friend in your life was not all that hidden, and if it was, it did not take much to put two and two together and come up with a three-dollar bill. Baron von Steuben's male relationships are on the record, and his monument stands in front of the White House. Alexander Hamilton's closeness with Col. John Laurens, the son of one of the members of the Continental Congress, was quite the talk of early 19th-century Washington. The talk of the town a few years later was the cohabitation of two senators—William Rufus de Vane King, who later became vice president under Franklin Pierce, and James Buchanan, Pierce's successor as president. The Lincoln White House had a "touch of lavender," as did one of America's greatest and most revered poets, Walt Whitman. The end of the century brought to light one of the most delightful revelations of the Washington social season when President Cleveland entertained an Indian princess of questionable gender.

The new century in D.C., as detailed in several preserved diaries, was loaded with clandestine meeting spots, theaters, and backroom clubs. The social clubs of the late 1800s eventually evolved into the bar scenes of the late 1900s, with many stories along the way. In the 1920s, when same-sex dancing was a back-room affair, there was a new musical on Broadway called *Irene*, featuring the song "Alice Blue Gown." This became the code tune a club singer performed to warn the boys in the back room that the cops were on the way in. The Harding administration had it all: a president with a mistress, the Teapot Dome scandal, a suicidal gay lover, and the Hope Diamond. Then J. Edgar Hoover eclipsed even that in a lovely ensemble. Beyond that scratched historical surface is a community perhaps more diverse than any. As

Anita Bryant said, "Homosexuality is nothing new," but the growth in visibility is. The community voices that fought to give women the right to vote were heard again and again in gay causes of non-discrimination and health. At first, mainstream America did not lift a finger for those dying of AIDS, a marginalized part of the whole community. It took marches, demonstrations, arrests, and quilts to cause action. Today, Gay Pride celebrations and different organizations truly show the diversity of a remarkable community, from the Mid-Atlantic Leather (MAL) weekend to the annual One in Ten Project's Reel Affirmations International Gay and Lesbian film festival. The most fascinating part of this tale is that the story is still playing out.

Images of America: *Gay and Lesbian Washington, D.C.* is the ultimate show-and-tell, with the responsibility of the teller to instill in the reader pride in our founding brothers and sisters. One will not get off the Metro at L'Enfant Plaza without thinking, "This name is part of gay history." Hopefully, many readers will be curious enough to read more on the subject—or at least search the Web for a topic that may only be touched upon here—and to consider what is between the lines of traditional history books. Indeed, there is pride in that discovery, and there is a community that is on the threshold. *Gay and Lesbian Washington, D.C.* is another image of America, a history out of the closet.

Author Frank Muzzy is pictured at the garden gate of the National Cathedral.

One
THE POLITICAL SIDE OF D.C.
"ABSTRACTED MANOR"

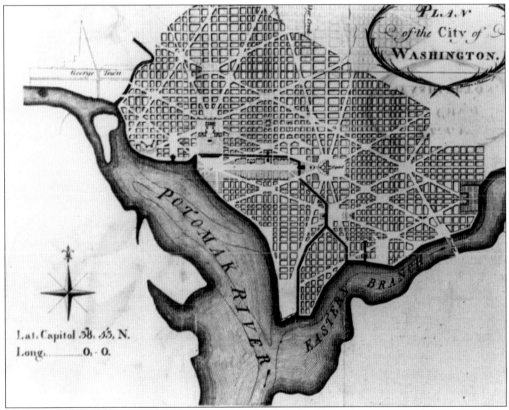

George Washington's protégé, Pierre L'Enfant, designed America's capital city. L'Enfant returned to America in 1784 with John Jacob Astor, and as a result of his introduction to New York society and the post-war building boom, his work flourished. He designed the manor of Alexander Hamilton, the Gracie Mansion at Hell Gate, and Astor's mansion. Astor also introduced him to Duncan Phyfe, and L'Enfant was soon exacting design fabrication for the cabinetmaker. Descriptions of L'Enfant were all the known euphemisms for homosexuals. He displayed "the artistic and fragile temperament," was "sensitive in style and dress," and as the First Federal Congress alluded, he had an "abstracted manner," not an architectural term. (Courtesy Library of Congress Prints and Photographs Division.)

When Baron von Steuben hired L'Enfant to illustrate the drill manual and, later, to design the insignia for the Society of Cincinnati, the Washington and L'Enfant connection was made. Over time, L'Enfant's plan was taken over by others and revised, but ultimately, the city reflected his design. Here, George Washington reviews the plans with L'Enfant of the new city on the Potomak (now Potomac) River, as depicted in the ceiling mural in south wing of the Capitol.

At this time, the place to be if you were gay or straight was New York. No eyebrows were raised on the discreet goings on of two men or women, especially in L'Enfant and von Steuben's social set. Nearly everyone in New York knew that L'Enfant was the protégé of Baron von Steuben.

Baron von Steuben came to America to train farmers at Valley Forge to be soldiers of the Continental Army. The troops were volunteer citizens who did not respond to discipline and who left the ranks when they felt they had contributed enough or had some farming to do. The officers, with a European view of commanding, placed emphasis on class distinction and distanced themselves from the soldiers. The Baron's approach put officers and soldiers on the same level. Whenever possible, they were to eat, drink, and sleep (platonically) with the soldiers. He wrote the drill manual adopted by the army, commanded a division at Yorktown, and was Washington's military planner following the war. Von Steuben's timing on the American scene could not have been better, and he departed Germany just ahead of the police, who were trying to arrest him for indiscreet behavior with several young men. On his passage, he brought with him a 17-year-old Frenchman to share his bed.

·MILITARY·INSTRVCTION·

This statue of Baron von Steuben is situated on the northwest corner of Lafayette Park. The base of the statue speaks volumes to military instruction. Many friendships were formed on other benches in this park in a similar manner. (Courtesy of Frank Muzzy.)

12

James Buchanan was the "Bachelor President," whose closet door, as indicated from history, was not that shut. He was engaged early on to Anne Coleman, who committed suicide after breaking off a two-week engagement. After serving as a congressman from Pennsylvania through the 1830s, he served as secretary of state under James K. Polk between 1845 and 1849 and was thought to become the next president. Instead, the nod went to Franklin Pierce. As a concession to Buchanan, the party offered the vice presidency to William Rufus de Vane King, his long-time companion. A bit effeminate, King wore long silk scarves and glittery accoutrements and was dubbed "Aunt Fancy." Andrew Jackson later referred to "Miss Nancy," King's nickname around Washington, as Buchanan's better half.

James Buchanan

"Buck" and "Nancy" shared apartments and homes together. When King was named ambassador to France, the frequent letters that crossed the Atlantic were small consolations. In one, King wrote, "Dear Buchanan, I am selfish enough to hope you will not be able to procure an associate who will cause you to feel no regret at our separation." Speculation is that it was a political orchestration and Buchanan, appointed Secretary of State, was left to occupy their home 1331 F St. NW and keet the home fires burning. (Courtesy of Martin Luther King Library, Washingtoniana Division.)

It is interesting to note that if Buchanan had gotten the nomination for President in 1844, it is likely that King would have picked up the second spot. Talk about your co-presidency! In his later years, Buchanan wrote that he was not the type to marry and did not need the company of a woman. He also wrote that if he did marry, it would be to find a companion to take care of him in his old age. (Courtesy of Library of Congress Prints and Photographs Division.)

There are stories of Lincoln that bristle mainstream historians, who seldom think of their subject in any other terms than asexual. Author Larry Kramer and others allude to much evidence of Lincoln's homosexuality and his life-long friendship with Joshua Speed. While a young man, Lincoln was traveling the back roads of Illinois and came upon a general store with a lone clerk. He asked the clerk if there were accommodations nearby, and the young, good-looking man offered to share his double-size bed. They shared this bed for the next four years. In Victorian times, it was not unusual for men to share a bed, but the correspondence, with references to the sweetness of Lincoln's kisses, stirred much speculation on the nature of this relationship. Regardless, their closeness in correspondence was life-long, seeking advice from one another and explaining decisions as to why they were taking wives. (Courtesy of National Archives.)

Kramer also suggests, in a 19th century "grassy knoll"–type theory, that Speed had introduced Lincoln to his assassin, John Wilkes Booth, the "most handsomest man in America." The "intimate reason" for the introduction was an additional catalyst for actor Booth's actions. (Courtesy of National Archives.)

The newest book about Lincoln's "streak of lavender," as Carl Sandburg put it, is *The Intimate World of Abraham Lincoln* by Dr. C.A. Tripp. It refers to Lincoln as a Kinsey 5 (on a scale 0 to 6), which means predominately homosexual but incidentally heterosexual. It takes into account his relationship with Speed as well as his relationships with some of his officers in the Union army. Daniel Derickson, captain of Lincoln's body-guard unit, often shared his bed in the White House when Mary Todd Lincoln was away. Apparently, the affair was common gossip around Washington high society. (Mathew Brady photo, courtesy of National Archives.)

Lincoln's poems and stories were rather ribald; some include anal references ("the egg it is laid") and slang for well-endowed ("low crotch"), which were explicit to homosexual relations in 19th-century America. (From Dr. C.A. Tripp's *The Intimate World of Abraham Lincoln*.)

> I will tell you a Joke about Jewel and Mary
> It is neither a Joke nor a Story
> For Rubin and Charles has married two girls
> But Billy has married a boy
> The girlies he had tried on every Side
> But none could he get to agree
> All was in vain he went home again
> And since that is married to Natty
> So Billy and Natty agreed very well
> And mama's well pleased at the match
> The egg it is laid but Natty's afraid
> The Shell is So Soft that it never will hatch
> But Betsy she said you Cursed bald head
> My Suitor you never Can be
> Beside your low crotch proclaims you a botch
> And that never Can serve for me
> —A. Lincoln

Peter Doyle was Walt Whitman's companion of 10 years. They met when Whitman came to Washington for a week and caught a streetcar near where the Air and Space Museum is today, on which Peter was the conductor. Doyle recalled, "We were familiar at once: I put my hand on his knee; we understood." Whitman's stay was extended. In the early part of the 1870s, Whitman resided near 14th and L Streets NW, but he previously worked in a series of hospitals around the city and lived in an equal number of rooming houses. Pictured here are Whitman and Doyle in Washington, D.C. in 1865. (Courtesy of Library of Congress Prints and Photographs Division.)

Peter Doyle was in Ford's Theatre the night Lincoln was shot. It is his recollections that Whitman used in his collection of poems *Leaves of Grass*. (Courtesy of Library of Congress Prints and Photographs Division.)

Matilda Coxe Stevenson was an anthropologist who worked in the West with Native Americans. She was sensationalized by an article in the *Illustrated Police News* as a fair, young, white woman who beat hostiles out west, which were untrue. The headline in March 1886 said, "An assassin red-devil cowed by white Mrs. Col. Stevenson of Washington, D.C., defeats an Indian assassination conspiracy in Arizona." (Courtesy of Library of Congress.)

Stevenson befriended a Native American princess named We'Wha. In 1886, she invited We'Wha to live in her home while the princess negotiated the Zuni tribal treaties with the government. Stevenson's home at 1303 P Street NW is pictured here.

The toast of the 1886 season, We'Wha was a frequent guest of the Speaker of the House and his wife and appeared before congressmen, Supreme Court justices, and the President at a gala charity benefit held at the National Theatre. In June, she visited the White House, and soon after, those passing by the south lawn were startled to see the six-foot princess weaving at her loom. It was later revealed that Princess We'Wha, who negotiated one of the best Indian treaties in U.S. history, was a man following the custom of the dual-spirited person. Living as a woman, she was revered by her tribe as the perfect person to negotiate treaties. Delighted by her D.C. hosts, she charmed them all with who she was—the first known drag queen (make that princess) in the White House. Here, We'Wha weaves on the grounds of White House in 1886. (Courtesy of Smithsonian Institute.)

All of Washington believed that We'Wha, the "berdache" (or dual-spirited) Zuni Indian, was a woman. She is pictured here in 1886. (Courtesy of National Anthropological Society.)

President Warren G. Harding's cabinet poses on the south lawn of the White House, c. 1921. Riddled with scandal, this Republican administration's diversity is evidenced in its cabinet. Harding's campaign manager and attorney general, Harry Daugherty (far right), often socialized with the first family, along with his companion, Jess Smith.

Smith and Daugherty shared a home at 1509 H Street NW, two blocks from the White House and just across from the most popular cruising spot for gay men in Washington, Lafayette Park. Pictured here, two men walk shoulder to shoulder down 15th Street, away from the park on the same block as the Smith-Daugherty home. (Used by permission of Historical Society of Washington, D.C.)

It was the fashion of the day with ladies of society to have male escorts, who were usually gay. Smith was the constant escort of First Lady Florence Harding. He helped select her flapper threads, along with her other constant companion, Evalyn Walsh McLean, the last private owner of the Hope Diamond. A bit of a dandy, Smith was often seen in a trademark bow tie and matching handkerchief, the hanky code of the day.

Smith's dealings at the nearby Shoreham Hotel (pictured in 1923 at H and 15th Streets NW) and his H Street home, as well as his boasting of connections with Washington insiders, were linked to the corruption of the Harding Presidency and the Teapot Dome Scandal. (Courtesy of the Library of Congress Prints and Photographs Division.)

Daugherty and Smith also shared a cottage in Ohio known as the "shack," as well as an apartment at the fashionable Wardman-Park Hotel. It was in that apartment that the much-publicized suicide of Smith occurred in May of 1923.

Having slept at the White House that night, Daugherty was not at home when Smith died. The police telephoned the President, who went to the guest room to inform his attorney general of Smith's death. Although ruled a suicide, there was much speculation. Smith was afraid of guns, so his choice seemed odd. His talk at the Shoreham Hotel indicated involvement in supplying booze to the White House during Prohibition, and with the other wrong-doings by the administration, he was certainly wanted out of town. Of course, there is always the curse of the Hope Diamond (although generally reserved for its owner): Smith, in his flamboyant manner, surely tried it on.

Jesse W. Smith Shoots Himself in Attorney General's Washington Apartment.

BROODED OVER ILL HEALTH

Had Been Store Owner in Ohio, but Followed Attorney General to Washington.

Special to The New York Times.

WASHINGTON, May 30.—Jesse W. Smith, for years a close companion of Attorney General Daugherty, and a personal friend of President Harding, committed suicide early this morning in the Attorney General's suite in Wardman Park Hotel, by shooting himself through the head with an automatic pistol. Lieut. Commander Joel T. Boone, nav medical aid at the White H˶˶˶˶ay Mr. Daugherty's phy˶˶˶˶ today in suicide ˶˶˶˶ckets. This will de ˶˶ property to the friend he admired so deeply, Mr. Daugherty, and to rela tives, principally in Washington Court House, Ohio, whence Mr. Smith came to this city not long before the advent of the Harding Administration.

23

In the Congressional Cemetery in southeast Washington, D.C., is the grave and family plot of J. Edgar Hoover. Nearby is the grave of his special friend, Clyde Tolson. There has been speculation as to what outfit the head of the FBI was buried in. It has been rumored that he cut quite a figure in ladies' garments in his private moments.

When Hoover, shown here, died in 1972, he left his entire estate to Tolson, along with the infamous secret files. Tolson lived three more years, never leaving the house except to visit Hoover's grave. It is said that mobster Sam Giancana had evidence of their relationship and used it to escape his life of shadows. (Courtesy of Library of Congress Prints and Photographs Division.)

Hoover, always surrounded by his favorites, is seen here celebrating New Year's with a group of friends.

Hoover (left) is pictured with his shuffleboard buddies, Royal Miller, Clyde Tolson, and Joseph McCarthy. Miller was often mistaken for Fred Mertz. (The Hoover files.)

The story goes that this anniversary portrait of Hoover was done as a surprise for Tolson, and it established a tradition that Hoover would dress up annually as a famous transvestite in history. (The Boudoir Portraits by "Hyacinth.")

Much has been made of Eleanor Roosevelt's relationship with Lorena Hickok, or "Hick" as she was called by ER. It did not seem to be anyone's business when the First Lady befriended the AP reporter who covered Franklin D. Roosevelt's run for the White House in 1932 or when the reporter moved into the White House. Mrs. Roosevelt became one of our most influential first ladies and went on to be the first U.S. delegate to the UN. (Courtesy of the Library of Congress Prints and Photographs Division.)

This statue of Eleanor Roosevelt is located at the FDR memorial in Washington, D.C.

The McCarthy hearings in Washington to root out communism in America seemed to house many closet cases, the biggest being Roy Cohn (right). (Courtesy of Library of Congress Prints and Photographs Division, *New York-World Telegram.*)

This series of images depicts the many faces of Roy Cohn. During the Army-McCarthy hearings, an attorney for the U.S. Army joked that when Cohn submitted a photo as evidence, it came from "a pixie . . . a close relative of a fairy." Cohn died in 1986 of AIDS-related complications.

Rep. Barney Frank is pictured addressing a GLBT meeting soon after he came to Washington, D.C., in 1988 and one year after he came out. Sen. Dick Armey once publicly made a "faux pas" calling him "Barney Fag." (Courtesy of Patsy Lynch.)

Today, Frank is one of the hardest-working members of Congress and a champion of the GLBT community. (Courtesy of Patsy Lynch.)

Bob Hasek of the Log Cabin Republicans—a national organization of gay Republicans—stands beside Congressman Jim Kolbe at a fund-raiser at Kolbe's home on Capitol Hill in 1998, shortly after the congressman came out of the closet. (Courtesy of Patsy Lynch.)

Dave Kopay (second from right) and Rick Rosendall, vice president of Gay and Lesbian Alliance (center) are pictured at the Anita Bryant candlelight protest in Dupont Circle. Kopay was a Washington Redskins football player who came out in response to a *Washington Star* report on homosexuality in sports. He became the accidental activist and ended up going against Anita Bryant, becoming a community voice. (Courtesy John Yanson.)

Two
COMMUNITY VOICES

This program was a souvenir from the first March on Washington. The visibility of the community went nationwide. Some were nervous that there would be a bad turn out; however, by the late summer, with advance word from across the country, it was clear that the march would be a large media-catching event, and its voice would be heard.

The many events that Washington has hosted, including the AIDS Quilt and the Gay March of 1979, have turned the eyes of the world to D.C. and brought much attention to these causes. Washington is playing the main stage, and these events serve to bolster the political strength of the gay and lesbian community nationwide. At the time, this banner reflected a movement, spearheaded by women, to flip the trend of having the male spin on gay causes. (Courtesy of Patsy Lynch.)

Gay women had marched down Pennsylvania Avenue before. There was a strong lesbian presence in the Suffrage Movement in general, as many worked tirelessly for the cause. It was the work of women such as Alice Paul and Lucy Burns that put together the march, 8,000 strong, during President Wilson's inaugural parade to draw attention to the disenfranchised. Note that women were not riding sidesaddle, but astride. (Courtesy Martin Luther King Library, Washingtoniana Division.)

Together, Alice Paul (upper left) and Lucy Burns (upper right), rented the back apartment at 1420 F Street NW, which consisted of three rooms. One was used as a large meeting room that held dozens of protesters, another served as their office, and a third was their living quarters. It was situated one block from the White House gate, where they held long and often freezing vigils to have a meeting with the President. It took seven more years from the march at Wilson's inauguration to ratify the 19th Amendment. (Courtesy of Library of Congress Prints and Photographs Division.)

Suffragettes stand vigil in protest in front of the White House, waiting for President Wilson to support the new amendment to give women the right to vote. (Courtesy of Library of Congress Prints and Photographs Division.)

Women of the Suffrage Movement pose in 1913 for a photo in front of their headquarters at 1420 F Street NW.

This unidentified woman shows off her marching costume, *c.* 1913. (Courtesy Library of Congress Prints and Photographs Division.)

In sharp contrast, another woman shows off her marching costume at the 2004 March for Women's Lives. (Courtesy of Mitzi.)

The Roadworks project, part of the womyn's music movement, created Sisterfire, the first urban women's music festival. Of course, men were invited. The festival was held every year in Takoma Park from 1982 to 1988. (Courtesy of Rainbow History Project and Amy Horowitz.)

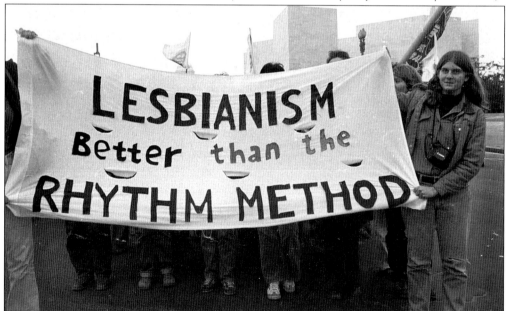

The importance of the strength of the women's community in Washington, D.C., has always been reflected in whatever causes with which they have aligned themselves. The Furies, a collective of lesbian separatists, are pictured at the Lesbian and Gay March of 1979. (Courtesy of Patsy Lynch.)

At this Supreme Court protest, these women hold a large net to capture, via performance art, all the negative terms that are applied to lesbians. (Courtesy of Patsy Lynch.)

The media stop to make the most of a photo op on the main stage that is Washington, D.C. (Courtesy of Patsy Lynch.)

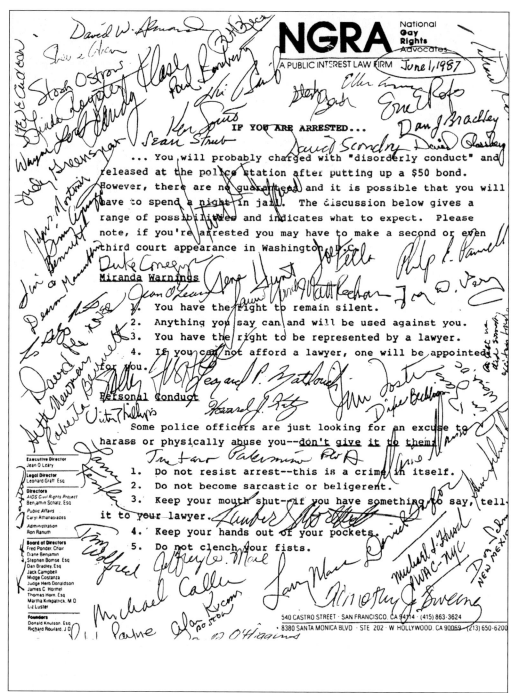

NGRA

National Gay Rights Advocates

A PUBLIC INTEREST LAW FIRM   June 1, 1987

IF YOU ARE ARRESTED...

... You will probably charged with "disorderly conduct" and released at the police station after putting up a $50 bond. However, there are no guarantees and it is possible that you will have to spend a night in jail. The discussion below gives a range of possibilities and indicates what to expect. Please note, if you're arrested you may have to make a second or even third court appearance in Washington, D.C.

Miranda Warnings

1. You have the right to remain silent.
2. Anything you say can and will be used against you.
3. You have the right to be represented by a lawyer.
4. If you cannot afford a lawyer, one will be appointed for you.

Personal Conduct

Some police officers are just looking for an excuse to harass or physically abuse you--don't give it to them.

1. Do not resist arrest--this is a crime in itself.
2. Do not become sarcastic or beligerent.
3. Keep your mouth shut--if you have something to say, tell it to your lawyer.
4. Keep your hands out of your pockets.
5. Do not clench your fists.

Executive Director
Jean O'Leary

Legal Director
Leonard Graff, Esq.

Directors
AIDS Civil Rights Project
Benjamin Schatz, Esq.
Public Affairs
Caryl Athanasiades
Administration
Ron Ranum

Board of Directors
Fred Ponder, Chair
Diane Benjamin
Stephen Bomse, Esq.
Dan Bradley, Esq.
Jack Campbell
Midge Costanza
Judge Herb Donaldson
James C. Hormel
Thomas Horn, Esq.
Martha Kirkpatrick, M.D.
Liz Luster

Founders
Donald Knutson, Esq.
Richard Roulard, J.D.

540 CASTRO STREET · SAN FRANCISCO, CA 94114 · (415) 863-3624
· 8380 SANTA MONICA BLVD · STE 202 · W HOLLYWOOD, CA 90069 · (213) 650-6200

This image is a portion of the mimeograph sheet signed by those arrested for the White House protest on June 1, 1987. Among them were Steve Endean, Jim Zais, Eric Rofes, Phil Pannell, Troy Perry, Jim Foster, Tim Sweeney, Judy Greenspan, Randy Klose, Jim Bennett, Deacon Maccubbin, Michael Callen, Jean O'Leary, Dan Bradley, and Leonard Matlovich. (Courtesy of Lambda Rising Archives.)

The first gay movement protest marches took place in 1965. Men and women dressed to look "employable," carrying picket signs at the White House and asking for full equality as U.S. citizens. Although gay men and lesbians worked in every government agency, they were fired if suspected to be gay. This early protest was conducted by 10 members of the Mattachine Society of Washington. (Courtesy of Bettmann Archives.)

"The Mattachine Society of Washington is a civil liberties social action organization, dedicated to improving the status of homosexual citizens through a vigorous program of action," said the society's formal statement of purpose. Mattachine, by all lawful means, worked to secure the basic constitutional rights of homosexual citizens and to eliminate adverse prejudice. It also cooperated with other organizations striving to realize full civil rights and liberties for all. The purpose of the group, it stressed, was not to act as an agency for personal introductions.

50¢

THE HOMOSEXUAL CITIZEN

NOVEMBER 1966

● NEWS OF CIVIL LIBERTIES
● AND SOCIAL RIGHTS
● FOR HOMOSEXUALS

FEATURE
Censorship

This image was taken at a meeting of national leaders at the 1965 East Coast Homophile Organizations Conference (ECHO). Clark Polak, standing second from the left, was the publisher of DRUM, the first men's magazine to feature frontal nudity. Shirley Willer, fourth from the left, was the national president of the first lesbian organization, The Daughters of Bilitis. Jack Nichols, fifth from the left, was vice-president of both the Mattachine Society of Washington and the Mattachine Society of Florida, Inc. Dr. Franklin Kameny, renowned gay civil rights activist, stands second from the right. (Courtesy of Jack Nichols.)

The Mattachine Society of Washington's first protest demonstration at the Pentagon took place in July 1965. Military policies in 1965 promised an undesirable discharge to any troop member suspected of being gay. Jack Nichols, on the far right, co-edited with Lige Clarke the nation's first gay weekly newspaper, GAY. (Courtesy of Kay Tobin Lahusen.)

In 1972, Jack Nichols and Lige Clarke were the first gay men to be interviewed by Geraldo Rivera. During that same year, Clarke and Nichols co-authored the first non-fiction memoir by a male couple, entitled I Have More Fun with You than Anybody. Starting in 1968, they wrote a popular weekly gay column in SCREW magazine. (Courtesy of Jack Nichols.)

Jack Nichols and Janet Welch attended a 1955 high school prom at the Shoreham Hotel. (Courtesy of Jack Nichols.)

Jan Welch is pictured with the boys of 1956. Jack Nichols is in the top row, center. Jan went on to work extending the women's Equal Rights Amendment and was the first open lesbian to be a president of a major chapter (Philadelphia) of the National Organization for Women. In the early 1970s, she coordinated a series of three groundbreaking programs for a local ABC affiliate called "Out Front." Since 1981, she has been the life partner of Alice Cohan. (Courtesy of Jack Nichols.)

Alice Cohan has the distinction of putting on the largest-ever event on the Mall with the March for Women's Lives on April 24, 2004. She is a woman for all our liberties. (Photo by Frank Muzzy.)

Jan and Alice enjoy a laugh together at a recent dinner party.

Mel Boozer, center, was both the first African-American and openly gay candidate to be put on a ballot for nomination for Vice President of the United States at the Democratic National Convention in 1980. During a moving speech, he said, "Would you ask me how I'd dare to compare the civil rights struggle with the struggle for lesbian and gay rights? I can compare, and I do compare them. I know what it means to be called a nigger. I know what it means to be called a faggot. And I can sum up the difference in one word: none." (Photo courtesy of the Lambda Rising archives.)

Marion Barry, a supporter of the gay community, stands at the Gay Pride street festival, held on S Street at Connecticut Avenue, trying on a "Kinsey 6" tee shirt for size. With him is Frank Kameny, who became the first openly gay person to campaign for national office with his run for Congress. The founder of the gay liberation movement in Washington, Frank Kameny worked as an astronomer with the federal government before he was fired in 1957 because of his sexual orientation. (Courtesy of *The Washington Blade*.)

Dawn Wilson speaks at a press conference at the first Transgender Lobby Day, October 2, 1995. Over 100 transgender-transsexual activists and supporters united from across the country to attend this coming-of-age of the transgender movement. Although covered by all major news outlets, the O.J. Simpson verdict pushed everything off the front page. (Courtesy of photographer/author Mariette Pathy Allen, from *The Gender Frontier*.)

Members of Transsexual Menace, Gay Men and Lesbian Opposing Violence (GLOV), Transgender Nation, and the National Gay and Lesbian Task Force (NGLTF) participate in a vigil for Tyra Hunter in front of Mayor Marion Barry's office on October 4, 1995. Reportedly, when the emergency personnel who were treating Tyra Hunter discovered she was a post-operative transsexual, they laughed, made inappropriate remarks, and perhaps did not give prompt care. The last comments made towards her before she died were the taunts of an insensitive society. (Courtesy photographer/author Mariette Pathy Allen, *The Gender Frontier*.)

Great idea, Suzie but WHERE?

Golly gee willikers, I think I wanna volunteer!

How about Volunteering at the Lesbian Services Program of Whitman-Walker Clinic?

LSP now has openings for peer counselors at the **Lesbian Resource and Counseling Center** (a Monday night rap group for lesbian and bisexual women).

LSP is hosting a Peer Counselor training on Saturday, November 14th at Whitman-Walker Clinic from 10 am to 4 pm.

As an LRCC volunteer you can learn, enhance and practice your skills in:
* Active Listening
* Group Facilitation
* Resource Counseling
* Crisis Intervention

PLUS! You can be a part of LSP's longest running volunteer driven support group!

so call Felicia at 202.939.7887 to sign up today!

Lesbian Services Program of Whitman-Walker Clinic
1407 S St., NW * Washington, DC 200009 * 202.939.7875

For nearly 15 years, the Lesbian Services Program (LSP) has improved health and wellness by providing medical care, mental health services, support groups, peer counseling, parenting support, health education and outreach, advocacy, and information and referral to our community. Created out of the Lesbian Health and Counseling Center of the late 1970s and supported by interested activists of the lesbian community, LSP was officially started by the Whitman-Walker Clinic in 1990. The Black Lesbian Support Group (BLSG), now a part of LSP for 15 years, began some two decades ago when a small group of African-American lesbians met in each others' homes for empowerment and support. LSP is now housed at 1810 14th Street NW after years of residing in the U Street corridor area of Washington, D.C. (Courtesy of Lesbian Services Program.)

One of LSP's campaigns was to encourage breast exams. Their slogan was "Touch your Breasts Often." (Courtesy of LSP.)

Scarlett's 22nd annual cake sale for charity is seen here in 1993 benefiting Food and Friends with sale and auction. Established in 1988, Food and Friends packages and delivers meals and groceries to people living with HIV/AIDS and other life-changing illnesses. Pictured here is Sister Carla, founder of Food and Friends, holding a cake up for bid with Michael Evans. Scarlett is the nickname of the gentleman who started the bake sale. (Courtesy of Frank Nowicki.)

Us Helping Us, an organization formed in 1985 by Rainey Cheeks, (right), Prem Deben, Aundrea Scott, and Howard Morris, held their first meetings at the Clubhouse, a now defunct Washington discotheque. Their main purpose is to provide HIV prevention and support services for the African-American community. (Courtesy of Max Robinson Center.)

Bishop Rainey Cheeks stands with Ruth Ellis, the oldest out lesbian at the time of the photo, celebrating her 100th birthday at the Black Pride Festival. (Photos by David Kosoko, courtesy of Clarence J. Fluker.)

Congresswoman Eleanor Homes Norton and Earl Fowlkes, coordinator of the festival since 1998, are pictured at the opening reception for D.C. Black Pride 2003.

The last year that Black Pride was held on Banneker Field was 1999. (Photos by David Kosoko, courtesy of Clarence J. Fluker.)

D.C. Black Pride 2001 was celebrated with a cruise down the Potomac on the *Odyssey*. Black Pride was originally a Memorial Day weekend tradition in D.C.'s African-American GLBT community. Between 1975 and 1990, they partied hard and celebrated the Children's Hour party at the Clubhouse bar (1296 Upshur Street NW) and stopped when the bar closed. In 1991, Black Pride was started up again by Welmore Cook, Theodore Kirkland, and Earnest Hopkins as a fund-raiser for HIV/AIDS in the black community. They also found support from local social clubs and bars, including the Encore Social Club, Best Friends, Hung Jury, Ziegfeld's, the Black Lesbian Support Group, and Faith Temple. The first event was an unqualified success, raising nearly $3,000 and drawing a crowd of 750 to 800 people.

Members of the Gertrude Stein Democratic Club, the voice of the GLBT community within the Democratic Party in the District of Columbia, march in the 1990 Gay Pride Parade. (Courtesy of Bob Dardano.)

Representing the gay conservative voice in the community, a group of gay Republicans formed the Walt Whitman Club in 1978, named for the poet who had lived in D.C. and supported Republican President Abraham Lincoln. In 1982, they were called the Capital Area Republicans. By the 1987 March on Washington, they called themselves the Log Cabin Federation. In 1989, the local chapter adopted the current name—Capital Area Log Cabin Club. They opened a national lobbying office in 1993, headed by Rich Tafel (center), the executive director. To his right is Robert Kabel, chairman, and to the left is neuroscientist lecturer and author Dr. Richard Cytowic. (Courtesy of Todd Franson.)

"Don't Ask, Don't Tell" was a Clinton compromise with Capitol Hill on non-discrimination in the military. Protesters argued, "It just does not work!" (Courtesy Earl Parker.)

A group of Empire Deaf Gays and Lesbians march in a 1979 parade and sign "I love you" to cheering crowds. The Washington GLBT deaf community is centered on Gallaudet University and the Capital Metropolitan Rainbow Alliance. CMRA was founded in 1977 at Jo-Anna's bar at 8th and E Street SE. (Courtesy John Yanson.)

Paulette Goodman of Parents and Friends of Lesbians and Gays (PFLAG) shows vintage signs at a recent talk sponsored by the Rainbow History Project on the rejected bus poster campaign. PFLAG is an important validation of the community, giving families and friends the love and understanding they deserve.

The applause for PFLAG is always louder and stronger than that for any other group at gay and lesbian parades. (Courtesy of Bob Dardano.)

Melissa Etheridge, Ellen and Betty Degeneres, Anne Heche, and friends gather at the Millennium March. (Courtesy of Hank Becker.)

These "Boys of LOC," otherwise known as the Library of Congress, who are often seen helping researchers review volumes of material for any number of reasons, take a day off to march with Pride in 1996. (Courtesy of Bob Dardano.)

This photo depicts press photographer Ward Morrison, a recorder of gay history, at the 2004 Gay Pride celebration on Pennsylvania Avenue. In the background, the gay men's chorus performs in front of the Capitol.

Patsy Lynch has captured the major events in the community for more than 25 years. Here, she is depicted at a recent exhibit of her political photography at Pulp on the Hill. (Courtesy of Luis Gomez.)

Under the guidance of Randy Shulman and a staff of dedicated photographers and reporters, *Metro Weekly* plays an important part in the GLBT community and catches the essence of weekly gay life in D.C. The cover of its premiere issue, published for May 5–11, 1994, is shown here. (Courtesy Randy Shulman, *Metro Weekly*.)

The *Washington Blade*, whose staff is shown here on October 31, 1991, started as the *Gay Blade* in 1969, working out of Frank Kameny's basement. They began by printing 500 copies of a one-page newsletter on a mimeograph machine to inform the gay community of its civil rights. (Photo by Doug Hinckle, courtesy of David Williams.)

Yes, it's the Sisters of Perpetual Indulgence in our nation's capital, encouraging the public to vote with consideration. Showing off, on her right hand, is the Hopeless diamond. (Courtesy of Todd Franson.)

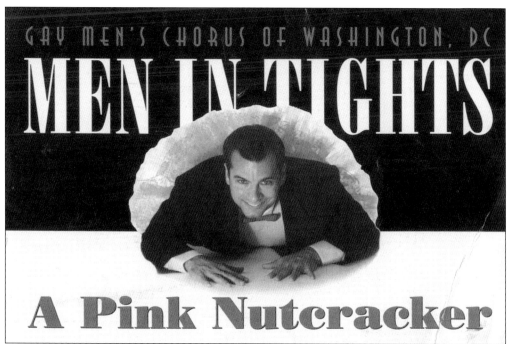

GAY MEN'S CHORUS OF WASHINGTON, DC

MEN IN TIGHTS

A Pink Nutcracker

The Gay Men's Chorus of Washington D.C., founded in 1981, is at the forefront of the gay and lesbian choral movement. This group affirms the community experience and promotes a culture through its musical excellence. They perform in venues, here and abroad, as diverse as the Kennedy Center, and as shown below, the annual Gay Pride festival.

This anti–gay marriage rally on the Mall, sanctioned by the Bush administration, was filled with rhetoric denouncing homosexuality and their attempts to gain equal rights and real domestic relationships. Without marriage, gays remain a segment of society who subsidizes the population both economically and socially. (Photo below, courtesy of Frank Muzzy.)

Anita Bryant, addressing the Save Our Children campaign, said, "Homosexuality is nothing new. Cultures throughout history have dealt with homosexuals almost universally with disdain, abhorrence, disgust—even death. The recruitment of our children is absolutely necessary for the survival and growth of homosexuality. Since homosexuals cannot reproduce, they must recruit, must freshen their ranks. And who better qualifies as a likely recruit than a teenage boy or girl who is surging with sexual awareness." The anti-adoption laws for gays in Florida are a legacy of Anita Bryant's campaign.

The Washington Hilton Hotel, sometimes referred to by locals as either the Reagan Hilton or the Hinckley Hilton, was the scene of the 1978 Anita Bryant protest. Nearly 3,000 people showed their displeasure at her speaking there. (Photo inset courtesy of John Yanson.)

Here are the ashes of Harvey Milk, the early gay activist and out San Francisco city supervisor, the first openly gay individual to be elected to public office. Milk, along with Mayor Moscone, was assassinated in 1978 by Dan White. Milk's ashes are kept in the vault at the Congressional Cemetery here in Washington, awaiting a final tribute and resting place. Sometimes, the community voices are silenced by hate. (Courtesy of Frank Muzzy.)

Leonard Matlovich (1943–1988) was also buried in the Congressional Cemetery. Proving that his activism would not be silenced by death, his epitaph reads, "When I was in the military they gave me a medal for killing two men—and a discharge for loving one." (Courtesy of Mike Elder.)

Three
"SILENCE = DEATH"

In June 1987 in San Francisco, a small group of people met to document the lives of the friends and lovers they had lost to the AIDS epidemic. They decided the upcoming Gay and Lesbian March in Washington seemed the appropriate venue to honor those who had died. At the same time, they wanted to get some much-needed political action about the crisis, since there was none. They organized the Names Project AIDS Memorial Quilt. On October 11, 1987, the first quilt showing included 1,920 panels. (Courtesy Patsy Lynch.)

Again in 1988, the quilt returned to the capital when the panels' number had increased to 8,288. Spread out and covering the Mall, the names were read aloud by celebrities, lovers, family, and politicians. Indeed, politicians were now were forced to utter the word AIDS. Above is the Ellipse on October 14, 1988; below is the AIDS quilt in 1992. (Above, courtesy of Patsy Lynch; below, courtesy of Earl Parker)

Camillo Wing Lee made his own quilt panel. He met Al Gore at the Names Project in Washington as Camillo helped others make panels for the AIDS quilt. Gore then looked at the project Camillo himself was working on and realized he was stitching his own panel. The final date on the panel reads 1997. (Courtesy of Todd Franson, *Metro Weekly*.)

On October 13, 1987, AIDS activists gather on the steps of the Supreme Court as part of the March on Washington for Gay Rights. At this protest, a sample of the first AIDS Quilt was delivered. (Courtesy of Patsy Lynch.)

Whoopi Goldberg, a strong activist in the AIDS struggle and for the GLBT community, helps a person with AIDS (PWA) on the streets of our nation's capital in 1987. (Courtesy of Patsy Lynch.)

In the photo at right, a man in the President's front yard tries to get the White House's attention for not being aggressive enough in the fight against AIDS. Reagan might as well have been in Santa Barbara that weekend. In the photo below, from left to right are Jean O'Leary of the NGLTF, Vic Baisel of Human Rights Campaign (HRC), and AIDS activists Don Bradley, Leonard Matlovich, and Reverend Perry. Together, they are bringing a wreath to the White House in 1987. (Courtesy of Patsy Lynch.)

In 1991, activists illustrate the result of public officials' lack of leadership in the AIDS crisis on the 10th anniversary of the first recorded case of AIDS (first known as Gay Related Immune Deficiency, or GRID). (Courtesy of Patsy Lynch.)

Patsy Lynch remembers police allowing this photo to be taken before they arrested Evan Underwood as the cake was wrestled to the ground. (Courtesy of Patsy Lynch.)

The dying wish of AIDS activist Steve Michaels was to have his funeral in front of the White House. So much of the inactivity in handling the AIDS epidemic rests with government officials, who are looked to for leadership. In contrast, in 1976 at a Philadelphia convention of the American Legion, a mysterious outbreak of pneumonia among attendees killed 34, and the government was mobilized to protect the citizenry. The same help was not allotted a few years later to a marginal segment of the population. Quite the opposite, instead, as our officials said, "It will rid us of the undesirables . . . fags and druggies." The next page shows a photographic essay by Patsy Lynch on that response.

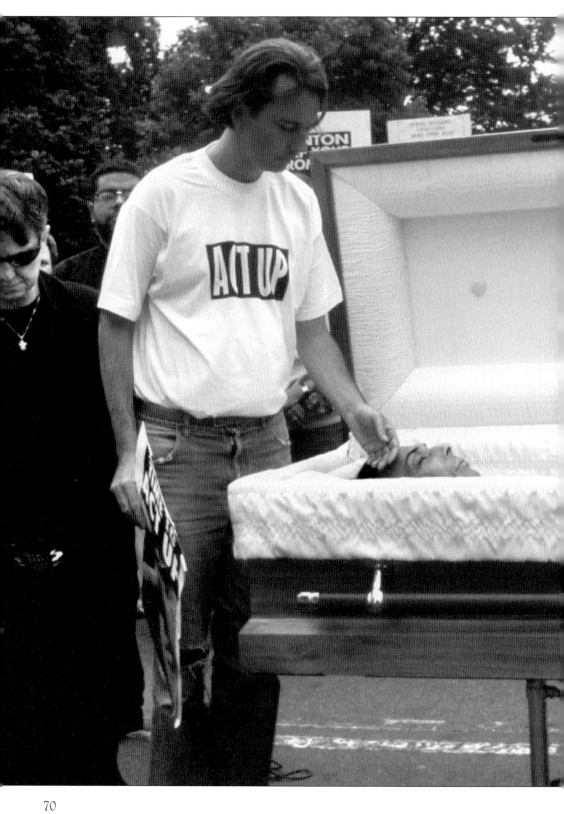

Steve Michael's funeral was held in front of the White House in 1995. (Courtesy of Patsy Lynch.)

An AIDS candlelight vigil was held around the Lincoln Memorial in 1989. (Courtesy of Patsy Lynch.)

A woman ponders the evening as her candle gives a visual echo of the Washington Monument. (Courtesy of Todd Franson, MW.)

The Whitman-Walker Clinic was established in 1973 to handle the gay and lesbian health issues of the DC area. With the advent of AIDS, WWC stepped up to become Washington's largest provider of HIV services. Its name is derived from Walt Whitman, America's foremost poet, and Dr. Mary Edwards Walker. Walker (1832–1919), disguised as a man, dedicated her efforts as a surgeon on the battlefield during the Civil War. She was awarded the Congressional Medal of Honor, and she proudly wore it every day. She found the strict guidelines for 19th-century women's dress ridiculous and instead wore men's attire, unfazed by predictable belittlement. (Courtesy Library of Congress Prints and Photographs Division.)

Walt Whitman, besides being a renowned American poet, worked in many D.C. hospitals as a health care worker during the Civil War years. (Courtesy of Library of Congress Prints and Photographs Division.)

The Whitman-Walker Clinic participated in the 1988 March on Washington. (Courtesy of Whitman-Walker Clinic.)

"Miracles can happen" is the theme of the lights on the Whitman-Walker Clinic, pictured on 14th and S Street NW on World Aids Day. Previously, the clinic was located in a church on Wisconsin Avenue in Georgetown; it later moved to Adams Morgan on 18th Street. (Courtesy of Whitman-Walker Clinic.)

President Clinton visits the clinic on World AIDS Day 2000. Pictured here with James Ball (center) and Executive Director Cornelius Baker (right), he was mainly there to listen and learn. He toured the facilities, met with clients, and drew attention to the importance of the clinic. There is complacency today; however, there is no cure, and the work must continue. (Courtesy of Whitman-Walker Clinic.)

Jamal administers an HIV test to Jesse Jackson at the Max Robinson Center of WWC in 2000. Though this may be a photo op, Jackson's celebrity indeed draws attention. (Photo by Denise Watkins, courtesy of Whitman-Walker Clinic.)

In 1993, Liz Taylor visits the medical center named for her, accompanied by Jim Graham (left). At the time, Graham was the executive director of Whitman-Walker; currently, he sits on the D.C .City Council. The Liz Taylor Medical Center, a part of the WWC, is an AIDS clinic and health center for AIDS victims. (Courtesy of Whitman-Walker Clinic.)

In the spring of 1996, Hillary Clinton and Mme. Bernadette Chirac paid a visit to the Whitman-Walker Clinic as part of a roundtable discussing women and HIV. Mme. Chirac is seen here talking with Whitman-Walker medical director Dr. Peter Hawley. (Courtesy of the Liz Taylor Medical Center.)

Pictured from left to right are David Burgdorf, Linda Minick, Dusty Cunningham, and Gary Dietrich, a.k.a. "Egypt." Dusty was the president of Whitman-Walker Clinic in 1984; he died in 1988. (Courtesy of David Burgdorf.)

Pictured at the AIDS Walk fund-raiser are Mayor Anthony Williams and members of D.C.'s city council. (Courtesy of Whitman-Walker Clinic.)

At Washington, D.C.'s annual AIDS Ride, the community rides bikes to raise dollars to continue the fight. (Courtesy of Max Robinson, center.)

Wallace Corbett (second from left) noticed that the African-American community was not well represented in the first AIDS Ride, so he formed Brother to Brother Sister to Sister United, (BBSSU.) Their presence grows yearly; they are now the largest black bike riding team in the area and have raised more than a million dollars. They are affiliated with the Max Robinson Center, which provides for AIDS/HIV services in Southeast D.C. The center was named for the first ever African-American network news anchor, who died of AIDS in 1988. Robinson hoped for more AIDS education and methods for its prevention, particularly in the black community. (Courtesy of BBSSU.)

Four

GAY MIGRATION

D.C.'s cruise spots have varied over its history. Their popularity depends on the success of the connections. Gentlemen, who were more at liberty to carouse due to social customs, usually met in out-croppings of nightspots and secluded parks. For ladies, it was the more refined atmosphere of nightclubs. In the early 20th century, one popular stretch for male cruising was between New York and Pennsylvania Avenues, along 9th Street and adjacent streets. Interestingly, the site chosen for J. Edgar Hoover's FBI building is on those same blocks (the man did not like to walk). Another popular spot was Lafayette Park across from the White House. Many gentlemen advertised their interests by wearing a smartly dressed suit, a bow tie, and a matching handkerchief flounced out of a pocket. Hats cocked to one side also indicated interest. Here, two men perhaps discuss a lunch-time tryst, otherwise known as a "nooner," at 11th and G Streets NW. (Courtesy of Library of Congress Prints and Photographs Division.)

As the 1940s filled D.C. with workers of wartime America and the military on leave, housing became both a problem and a delight. This photo from the *Washington Star Press* is a set-up shot to emphasize the bed shortage at the time.

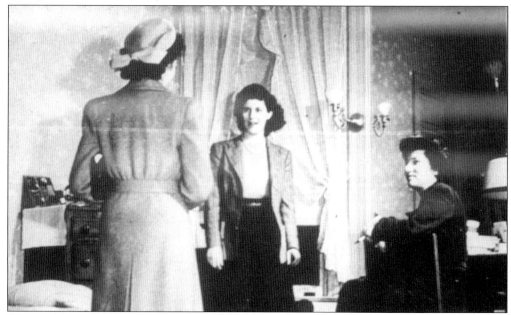

Women often rented extra rooms to other women as the increase of female workers poured into Washington to replace the declining male work force. This helped create a stronger lesbian community, later evidenced in the 1950s, 1960s, and 1970s. New York became the seat of gay activism, while Washington was the center of for the lesbian community. (Photos by Esther Bubley, courtesy of Library of Congress Prints and Photographs Division.)

A citizen's patriotic duty was clear. If a sailor was on leave and sitting on the iron rail on the side of the Willard Hotel at 14th and Pennsylvania NW (shown below), he'd receive Washington hospitality. He would be taken home, fed a home-cooked meal, and offered the guest room. In the 1940s, this became a number-one pick-up spot in D.C. for our boys in uniform.

In the late 1960s, gays began moving into Georgetown, which contained gay-friendly establishments like The Georgetown Grill and Mr. Henry's on Wisconsin Avenue. The nearby intersection of Dumbarton and 31st Street, with its popular lamppost, became the number-one cruise spot in D.C. In 1972, residents' complaints prompted police to begin harassing gays. The Gay Activist Alliance (GAA) was formed when a group of citizens visited the police chief. After waiting all day, they were told he was gone and to leave. They refused and were arrested for breaking and entering. In court, the judge declared the demonstrators guilty but said he would have done the same thing. Weeks later, the chief finally met with the GAA. When Georgetown experienced an increase in crime, residents asked police to leave the cruisers alone. As long as the streets were full, criminals stayed away. Among those arrested was Deacon Maccubbin, who, in 1974, contributed to the migration of gays into Dupont Circle. He opened a gay bookstore called Lambda Rising at 1724 20th Street NW, housed in a building with the D.C. switchboard, social services, and a shop called Earthworks. Lambda Rising was a discrete shop for gays to frequent: upon entering the building, no one knew to which space you were headed, a comfort for a society still in the closet.

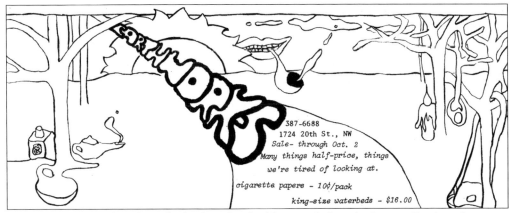

This ad is for Earthworks, which shared a building with Lamda Rising. Earthworks was a paraphernalia shop that claimed to have everything but the weed.

The first Lambda Rising was 300 square feet and contained 250 gay titles. It was 1976, and that was nearly everything that was available. They outgrew the space in a year. Today, there are over 20,000 titles available. (Courtesy of Lambda Rising Archives.)

Lamda Rising moved in 1977 from 20th Street to a much larger space on S Street NW.

On opening day at 2012 S Street NW, people were at first concerned that the unshaded windows would be too much exposure. However, the open windows represented a coming out for both store and customer. With Lambda as the destination, gay foot traffic followed down P Street to Dupont Circle and over to S Street. Soon, more places catering to gays opened up along the route. (Courtesy of Lambda Rising Archives.)

Deacon Maccubbin stands with husband Jim Bennett in 1984 in Lambda Rising's new store at 1625 Connecticut Avenue.

Andy Warhol, not in costume, makes an appearance at a Halloween book signing at Lambda Rising on October 31, 1985. (Photo by Patsy Lynch courtesy of Lambda Rising Archives.)

Along the migration trail on P Street, many of the existing neighborhood bars became gay establishments, and the famous P Street Beach was well on its way to being the cruisiest spot of the day.

It is in this area that the first D.C. Gay Pride festival was planned, held in a schoolyard adjacent to the P Street Beach. One of the first organizers on the scene was Deacon Maccubbin, pictured pre-Lambda Rising on the left with a friend.

This program was created for the first Gay Pride festival in 1972. The two previous years, the community went to New York for the Stonewall anniversary. Now, D.C. would host its own and hold events in several areas around the city. There were free gay movies at the Metropole Cinema at 411 L Street NW, a dance and art show at the GAA Community Center at 1213 13th Street NW church service and picnic at P Street Beach, and "happenings" at Lafayette Park. (Courtesy of the Lambda Rising archives.)

Regina, a.k.a. "Disco Granny," was a festival icon through the 1970s. She never missed Gay Pride and was always gaily attired. Here, her buttons read, "Think straight, be gay" and "Old fairies never die, they just blow away!" (Courtesy of John Yanson.)

Today, Gay Pride is one of the biggest festivals in the city. During the festival, a parade snakes through the neighborhoods, and a giant Pennsylvania Avenue block party with booths and entertainment keeps D.C. rocking through the weekend. With connected events, Gay Pride kicks off the summer in Washington, D.C. At the 2004 Gay Pride festival, author Frank Muzzy (right) embraces his special friend, Mike Elder.

A beaded Mayor Tony Williams celebrates a more diverse community at the annual Gay Pride parade. The Mayor's Office of GLBT Affairs serves as the liaison to the Executive Office of the Mayor and other agencies that provide services and community outreach, as well as provide information on policy and research issues that affect the local GLBT residents of the District of Columbia.

At the 1993 D.C. Gay Pride parade are Dick McHugh, second owner of the D.C. Eagle and his yellow Packard convertible, with Frank Nowicki (center), Mr. Mid-Atlantic Leather; Tony Wilging, Mr. DC Eagle; and Jose Ucles, Mr. American Leatherman. (Courtesy of Frank Nowicki.)

Dykes on Bikes, in the 1994 Pride parade, are coming down 16th Street from Meridian Hill Park. (Courtesy of Bob Dardano.)

Luke Sissyfag stands at Gay Pride in 1994. Sissyfag was born Luke Montgomery but became an AIDS activist, changed his name, interrupted President Clinton's speech on World Aids Day 1993 at Georgetown University, ran unsuccessfully for mayor of Washington D.C., reportedly became an anti-gay Christian in Seattle, and fizzled out of sight. (Courtesy of Bob Dardano.)

A group of Radical Fairies celebrate the May Day ritual in Dupont Circle, 1995. The Radical Fairies got their start in 1978 in California and have since spread homo-hippie joy to all corners of the country. (Courtesy Frank Asher.)

ANNIE'S

ANNIE'S PARAMOUNT
STEAK HOUSE
SINCE 1948
AND
STILL RUNNING

The gay population migrated east from Dupont Circle to the next commercial district of 17th Street with the opening of several clubs and restaurants. Annie's was originally located up the block where JR's is now, but it is well established at its present location. It has become that comfortable spot between the bars on 17th to relax with new friends and run into old ones. Here, the real Annie graces the cover of her menu.

Ron Henderson came to Washington, D.C., in 1987 with the first AIDS Quilt. He was part of the group who honored men who had died of the disease by laying a quilt before the legislators on the Nation's Mall. They also brought a small section to the Supreme Court for protest. The following year, he and other demonstrators laid that same quilt before the Food and Drug Administration asking for the early release of experimental drugs in hopes that those dying with HIV/AIDS might have a chance of survival. Ron, above on the right with Dr. David Moulton, climbed on top of the bus to protest and wait to be arrested. "We needed a ladder, and there one was on the side of the FDA building. It was so cold, someone threw the Quilt up to us and we wrapped ourselves in it. We *used* the Quilt to keep us warm," said Ron in an interview. (Courtesy of Patsy Lynch.)

This 1988 banner says, "The Names Project: we are your sisters and brothers, sons and daughters, fathers and mothers, friends and lovers, neighbors known and neighbors unknown . . . you, me." (Courtesy Patsy Lynch.)

Sixteen years later, Ron marches for women's lives on the Mall. He helped lead the gay migration across the northwest section of D.C. to 14th Street and Logan Circle, with his card, gift, book, and art store Pulp. The commercial district on 14th had never really recovered from the 1968 riots until shops moved in, led foremost by Home Rule, Go Mama Go, and Pulp. The area is now a hub of activity, gay and straight. Theater, furniture and clothing stores, gardening stores, and outdoor restaurants fill the blocks.

Pulp's first location was temporary, up some steep stairs and above a market next door in an old beauty salon, where the sinks and hair dryers were used for for display. Pictured in November 2002, from left to right, are Ron, Christine, Reggie, and Reggie's mother Gail. (Courtesy of Frank Muzzy.)

Pulp on 14th Street, with a second location on Capitol Hill, is the hub of new activity for the neighborhood. Their mottos are the same: "Come feel the love." (Courtesy of Mitzi.)

Logan Circle, a residential circle, and Shaw, the neighborhood to the east, seem to be the most recent phase of gay migration in the northwest quadrant, although there is now a vibrant out-of-the-closet community throughout D.C. Capitol Hill has had an established gay community for generations. Also, the meeting places on 8th Street SE, Barracks Row, and Pennsylvania Avenue and the surrounding neighborhoods have a rich gay history extending back several decades.

In 1993, Brad Harris and Paul Somner took some inspiration from Chicago's Pink Pages and put together one of the first gay phone directories. The first printing was 80 pages, with 25,000 copies. Today, the Other Pages contains 300 pages and distributes 50,000 copies, with sister editions in Philadelphia (the Freedom Pages) and in Baltimore (the Charm City Other Pages.) The current issue has the added terminology "queer" in hopes of being more inclusive of the lesbian, gay, bisexual and transgender community.

Five

GATHERING PLACES
"THE GAYS OF OUR LIVES"

Social clubs, the forerunner of today's bars and organizations, were the meeting places for gay men in the 1880s. Gay life in Washington, D.C., was scarcely common knowledge among friends and family. In some cases, diaries were found in personal papers and secrets, if not destroyed, were revealed. The book *Jeb and Dash* captures gay life between 1918 and 1945 and is the result of one family caring for that history. Jeb noted his favorite bench in the park and the theaters and beaches and other meeting spots of gays. Jeb and Dash are pictured here. (Courtesy of author Ina Russell.)

B.F. Keith's Theatre, a vaudeville house at 619 15th Street, was a meeting place or hangout for gays in the 1920s, 1930s, and 1940s. Old Ebbitt's Grill stands on this location today. (Courtesy of Library of Congress Prints and Photos Division.)

In 1975, the Metropole Cinema Club was the place to catch a movie and a "date for the evening," featuring such films as *Back Row* and *Boys in the Sand* with Casey Donovan and *Black Heat*, the first gay film with a black cast. (Courtesy of the Rainbow History Project.)

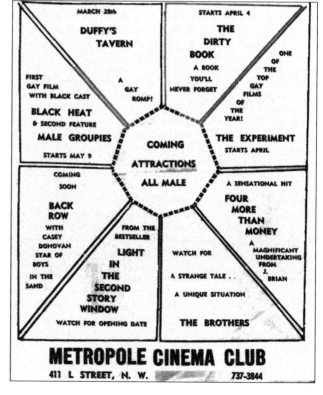

Dr. John Moore McCalla was a bisexual man whose writings, which still survive, are a window into the late 1800s. In 1866, he helped found the Misanthrope Club, whose members were largely bisexual or homosexual. Members included such prominent individuals as John A. Baker and Seaton Munroe, who founded the Metropolitan Club; John Franklin, attorney and organist of St. Paul's; Eugene Phillippe Jacobson, Congressional Medal of Honor winner; and Col. W.G. Moore, private secretary to Abraham Lincoln and Andrew Johnson and superintendent of district police from 1886 to 1898. (Courtesy of Ted Goldsborough.)

The doctor lived in the heart of Washington, D.C., in a home at 820 17th Street NW, just blocks from Lafayette Park, the central cruise park of the city. This stereograph of the park is from the 1870s. Whatever could these gentlemen be discussing? (Courtesy of Library of Congress Prints and Photographs Division.)

This house at 820 17th Street was built by McCalla in 1886 for his family. (Courtesy of Ted Goldsborough.)

The first black social clubs were Best of Washington Social Club, 5+5, and the Associates, formed in the late 1970s. They answered some of the discrimination blacks faced in bars and were opened to both men and women in the black community. John Robinson, above left, founded 5+5, which stood for 5 men and 5 women, on October 26, 1979. W. Robert "Bob" Lomax, above right, was one of the founders and president of the Best of Washington Social Club. These clubs often planned dances in hotels and picnics, but they also sponsored charity works. (Photos courtesy of Buddy Sutson.)

Be Be Garth, manager of the largely drag African-American bar Bachelor's Mill, stands with Buddy Sutson, one of the founders of the Best of Washington Social Club.

At the Alice Awards, the best nightspot, best club affair, best-dressed person, best bartender, most congenial person, and couple of the year were named by the Best of Washington Social Club. One person each year also won an award for dedication to outstanding service to the community.

LaZambra, a restaurant that operated from 1970 to 1985 at 1406 14th Street, was named nightspot of the year in 1979 by the Best of Washington Social Club. (Courtesy of Rainbow History Project.)

The Lodi at 918 17th Street, another basement bar, opened in 1935 and closed soon after this photo was taken in the early 1950s as the whole block was razed for development. Brett Beemyn, with The Rainbow History Project, remembered, "You walked in and there was this Jewish woman from New York. She liked to sing Yiddish songs. A heavy-set black women, she must have weighed 200 pounds, would be there on alternate nights." (Courtesy of the Martin Luther King Library.)

A former horse barn in the 1800s, Omega stands tucked away in an alley off P Street west of Dupont Circle and catered to a broad cross-section of D.C.'s gay community. In its previous incarnation, Omega was known as the Fraternity (or "Frat") House from 1976 to 1997. Over the years they have hosted nude dancers, karaoke, an upstairs leather club, "Sorority Night" for women, and "Diva Las Vegas," a Monday night drag show. (Photo by Mitzi.)

Prior to closing in 2004, Nob Hill was the oldest continuously operating bar in D.C. and was one of the oldest African-American gay bars in the country. Nob Hill opened first as a private club from 1953 to 1957 and then continued as one of the major drag show venues. (Courtesy of Rainbow History Project.)

Phase One is currently the oldest continuously operating gay or lesbian bar in D.C. Phase One has long been one of the principal women's bars in the District. It opened in 1971 next door to the Plus One, where gay owners Henry Hecht (of the department store family), Donn Culver, and Bill Bickford broke the "no same-sex dancing" code by installing a dance floor. Its popularity and money-making ability ensured that the dance would continue. (Courtesy of Mike Elder.)

Tracks, the popular club from 1984 to 1999, offered dancing and hosted many top acts of the day. Always a crowd pleaser, the Village People, somehow surviving their film debut in *Can't Stop the Music*, appear to be having trouble spelling "Y.M.C.A." (Courtesy of the *Washington Blade*.)

These are tickets for *Broadway Forever* at Tracks. (Courtesy of Ann Wachtel, former house manager.)

METRO WEEKLY

MW

SEPTEMBER 25, 1997

IT'S A GOOD LIFE: MR. HENRY AT 80

SNAPSHOTS: MAUTNER AND AIDS WALK... SCHROEDER'S NEW SERIES...
ALEVIZOS ON PEACEMAKER... SHULMAN ON 69... BUGGED IN MIAMI

In 1966, Henry Yaffe founded the first, and now the last, of the Mr. Henry's restaurants on Capitol Hill. They dotted the city for years and were known for their gay-friendly atmosphere. It was at his Georgetown location that he first promoted Roberta Flack, then a schoolteacher, as a singer. Liberace and Woody Allen came to hear her when she performed at Mr. Henry's on the Hill, in what is now the Roberta Flack room. (Courtesy Randy Shulman, MW.)

MCC Washington was founded by Rev. J.E. Paul Breton as the Community Church of Washington, originally meeting in his home. Meeting for 9 years at 415 M Street starting in 1984, it was the model for other congregations around the country. Above is the new home, opened on December 17, 1992, with 500 members. (Courtesy of Mike Elder.)

The Christmas concert was the first event in the new church and is an annual must to welcome in the season and the loving community that it serves.

The DC Eagle history has its origins in the Spartan MC motorcycle club and Louis's, a bar on 9th Street across from the FBI headquarters. Don Bruce, one of the early presidents of Spartan MC, decided that the club needed its own bar, so he and his brother, Eddie, pooled their money and opened the first of three DC Eagles at 904 9th Street NW. The night before it opened, Don held a ceremony and invited members of the Spartan MC to place nails into a sculpture of an eagle behind the bar. It remained as a symbol until the new convention center (now also gone) was built on this site. (Courtesy of DC Eagle Archives.)

Don Bruce owned DC Eagle from 1971 to 1987. (Courtesy of DC Eagle Archives.)

Here is DC Eagle on 7th Street NW, with bikes lining the street during the Biker Brunch in 1985. The building also housed the original Leather Rack clothing store and an acclaimed restaurant with write-ups in *Washingtonian Magazine*. The next move was in May 1987 to its present locale in the old Manhattan Transfer Company building. The building is also the site of the only operating hand crank elevator left in the city. (Courtesy of DC Eagle Archives.)

Here is the Spartan MC in 1985. (Just say "Oh!") (Courtesy of David Burgdorf.)

Tinsley Halter Cunningham III, a.k.a. Dusty, was the president of Whitman-Walker Clinic. He became a Spartan in 1986. (Courtesy of David Burgdorf.)

This gathering celebrated the 25th anniversary of the Centaur MC, one of the original leather clubs in D.C. (Courtesy of Centaur MC archives and Danny Linden.)

Dick McHugh owned DC Eagle from 1987 to 2001. (Courtesy of DC Eagle archives.)

This tribute to DC Eagle owner Richard McHugh occurred in August 2000. (Photo Michael Wichita, courtesy *MW*.)

The popularity of the social clubs of the late 19th century seemed to diminish as the acceptance of gay bars grew. Organizations and fraternal clubs developed as an extension of the bar scene, catering to a diverse community. The bear community was a counter to the sleek "stand and model" crowd and appeared in D.C. in the mid-1990s with two main groups: the Chesapeake Bay Bears and the DC Bear Club (DCBC).

The Bear flag, designed in 1995 by D.C.'s Craig Byrnes, is a bear paw on a field of multi-colored stripes representing fur. Colors of bears now identifies hundreds of bear clubs in the U.S. and worldwide. (Courtesy of Charlie Hopwood.)

The club logo in the inset was designed in 1993 by David Williams; the updated logo was displayed 1996 on the parade banner. (Courtesy of Charlie Hopwood.)

DCBC, the District of Columbia Bear Club, was founded in 1995 to promote fellowship among Bears, Cubs, Levi-Leather, and other diverse members of the gay and lesbian community. (Courtesy of DCBC and John Copes, President)

Pictured are Mr. Bear Pride with a DC Bear Cub. The bear run is held each year in November with the purpose of connecting with old friends and meeting new. The DCBC event is known as the friendliest run around.

The District of Columbia Bear Club marches in the Gay Pride Parade with Mr. DC Bear Invader. (Courtesy of DCBC.)

In 1991, Phil Hastings, Phil Riggin, Mike Lentz, and Dave Hehr founded the Atlantic States Gay Rodeo Association. Within three months, they were holding "the spirit of the West" here in D.C., with rodeo events, seminars, social activities, and monthly trail rides. This poster was from its first year.

The crowds come out in 1992 to watch the wranglers on the field (and to do a little wrangling in the stands as well). (Courtesy of David Burgdorf.)

The Atlantic Stampede, otherwise known as the Gay Rodeo, is an annual event anticipated by the cowboys and cowgirls of Washington, D.C., as well as all who just love chaps. (Photos by Patsy Lynch.)

The gay rodeos across the nation in the early 1970s were difficult to produce, as those who would have supplied the calves, steers, and horses did not want to provide gays with their animals. This photo, taken by notable D.C. photographer Patsy Lynch, documents the action of the rodeo as this woman gets the thrill of the ride. Gay photographer Ward Morrison captures another angle.

Remington's has been the country-western meeting place for many years. Early on, before its expansion into the building next door, the club had a 10 by 10–foot floor for dancing, which sort of eliminated a lot of the slide movements in doing the two-step. The D.C. style was more up and down in two-stepping.

Washington's own DC Cowboys, a dance troupe and calendar boys, was formed in 1999. A little bit cowboy and a little bit Broadway, DC Cowboys today make appearances for many benefits and fundraisers, Gay Pride, the IGRA Rodeo, and country-western dance clubs across the nation and Canada. (Courtesy of DC Cowboys.)

"Results, the Garage" was the origin of the health club that has been so important to the community. Here, Doug Jefferies planted the seed that is now Results, the Gym. At right is Results, the Gym, at their first official location on R and 17th Streets NW.

Doug Jefferies and some of his colleagues are pictured at Results, Dupont Circle, soon after their move to the U Street location. Here, they became an important part of neighborhood growth and were integral to the gay and lesbian community.

The second location of Results, the Gym, was on Capitol Hill, and it serves gay and straight families of the community. (Courtesy of the Results Archives.)

The D.C. soccer team Federal Triangles is a member of the International Gay and Lesbian Football Association. They were organized for charitable and educational purposes to encourage players, gay and gay-friendly, at all levels to participate and improve their skills with local, national, and international league play. (Courtesy of Barrett Brick.)

In 2001, six members of the Washington team competed with several Mid-Atlantic members to defeat the United Europe team 2-1 in a hard-fought match. They collected the Men's Division II IGLFA bronze medal.

We'Wha was quite the sensation in Washington, D.C., in 1886 when she appeared at the National Theatre before the powerful politicos. Of course, they had no idea of her dual spirit. She is, in today's terms, one of the first recorded drag queens in D.C. More contemporary drag has many grande dames. (Photo courtesy of Library of Congress Prints and Photographs Division.)

Mame Dennis (Carl Rizzi), drag queen extraordinaire of the House of Beekman Place, has been entertaining D.C. audiences since the 1960s. (Courtesy of Frank Nowicki.)

In 1961, "Liz Taylor" started the first safe haven for female impersonators in the D.C. area. Wearing drag was not illegal in D.C., unlike in surrounding states, but it was an invitation to harassment, physical attacks, and other forms of discrimination. By creating an organized home for female impersonators, "Liz Taylor" provided security, social events, and mentoring. Called The Academies, it grouped a number of houses, including Henry Street, Beekman Place, Butterfield 8, and others. (Photos Courtesy of Frank Nowicki.)

Rayceen Pendavis of the house of Pendavis performs currently at Club Lulu's, a straight club. This drag family, noted in the film *Paris is Burning*, has D.C. roots. (Photo by David Kosoko, courtesy of Clarence J. Fluker.)

The Brass Rail started as a New York–style restaurant in the 1960s at 517 9th Street. It later moved to 809 and eventually 811 13th Street. It had been a biker bar and a country western club, but it became one of the main African-American drag bars. Also, as is tradition in so many gay establishments, it moved from a basement bar to upstairs. By 1973, the Railettes were one of the in-house entertainment groups. (Courtesy of Rainbow History Project.)

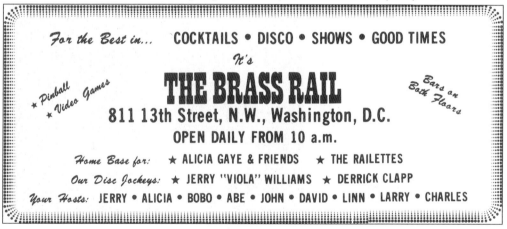

Ziegfields enters the 1992 gay parade in style, with "Miss Ella Fitzgerald," assisted by her entourage, greeting her fans. (Photo by Bob Dardano.)

"Ella Fitzgerald" has been performing since the 1980s. (Courtesy of Frank Nowicki.)

The mix of the leather and drag communities is seen here. Sometimes girls just want to have fun. In this photograph, the Kinsey Sicks (from left to right, Trixie, Winnie, Rachel, and Trampolina) perform at Mid-Atlantic Leather (MAL), complete with leather armbands. (Courtesy of Frank Nowicki.)

The DC Kings from King Kalendar 2005, from left to right, are (front row) Peter Dicksen, Ken Vegas, and Allix Allot; (back row) Jake Badger, Noah Rex, and E-Cleff in Washington, D.C., before a performance at Liquid Ladies at APEX. Yes, they are "packing." The Kings have been a drag mainstay in the District since 2000, continuing a performance tradition stretching back to the 1930s. (Courtesy of Sophia Piellusch.)

The annual Miss Adams Morgan Pageant, held ever year since 1987 during the Gay High Holy Days of Halloween, celebrates the most outrageous thematic drag. The organizers, the Dupont Social Club, do not allow the media to cover the event and instead videotape it themselves. Here is Miss Lobster Girl pleasing a formal crowd. (Courtesy of Fraülein Blaue.)

Another Halloween must is the annual High Heel Race down 17th street. These girls are celebrating with the other contestants, some of who are vicious in stilettos while others do it in style. (Courtesy of Frank Asher.)

Here's a toast to the diversity of Washington's gay, lesbian, bisexual, and transgender community! (Courtesy of Ward Morrison.)